LEARNING ABOUT

Trees

Catherine Veitch

Chicago, Illinois

The author would like to dedicate this book to her mother, Jacqueline Veitch, who inspired her with a love of nature.

Edited by Dan Nunn, Rebecca Rissman, and Sian Smith
Designed by Joanna Hinton-Malivoire
Picture research by Mica Brancic
Production by Sophia Argyris
Originated by Capstone Global Library Ltd
Printed and bound in China by South China Printing Company Ltd

17 16 15 14 13
10 9 8 7 6 5 4 3 2 1

Library of Congress Cataloging-in-Publication Data
Veitch, Catherine.
Learning about trees / Catherine Veitch.—1st ed.
p. cm.—(The natural world)
Includes bibliographical references and index.
ISBN 978-1-4109-5402-2 (hb)
ISBN 978-1-4109-5407-7 (pb)
1. Trees—Juvenile literature. I. Title. II. Series: Natural world (Chicago, Ill.)
QK475.8.V45 2013

582.16—dc23   2012049393

Acknowledgments
The author and publisher are grateful to the following for permission to reproduce copyright material: Alamy pp.4 inset top (© Bob Gibbons), 8 main (© CuboImages srl/Paroli Galperti); FLPA pp.4 main (© Bob Gibbons), 5 inset bottom (Martin B Withers), 8 inset, 19 inset bottom (Marcus Webb), 16 main (Derek Hall), 19 inset top (Minden Pictures/© Adri Hoogendijk); Nature Picture Library pp.9 main (Mike Read), 16 inset bottom (© Simon Colmer); Photoshot pp.12 main (© NHPA/Kevin Schafer), 20 inset (© Cuboimages/Paroli Galperti), 20 main (© Photos Horticultural/Michael Warren), 23 flower (© Cuboimages/Paroli Galperti); Shutterstock pp.4 inset bottom (© Grigorii Pisotsckii), 4 inset top (© Ewa Studio), 5 main (© Chuck Cho), 6 (© Oleg Znamenskiy), 7 inset (© Tamara Kulikova), 7 main (© EastVillage Images), 9 inset (© marlee), 10 inset bottom (© Radka Palenikova), 10 inset top (© tolchik), 10 main (© Martina I. Meyer), 11 (© Maksym Gorpenyuk), 12 inset (© Julie Simpson), 13 inset (© William Berry), 13 main (© Zack Frank), 14 inset (© Nastya22), 14 main (© kosam), 15 inset (© Brandon Bourdages), 15 main (© Yusia), 16 inset top (© Sergej Razvodovskij), 17 inset (© Robyn Mackenzie), 17 main (© Konrad Weiss), 18 inset and main (© Alessandro Zocc), 19 main (© marilyn barbone), 21 inset (© Frank L Junior), 21 main (© Jeff Dalton), 22 bark (© EastVillage Images), 22 berry (© marlee), 22 blossom (© Ewa Studio), 22 branch (© marilyn barbone), 23 bud (© haraldmuc), 23 catkin (© Sergej Razvodovskij), 23 cone (© Alessandro Zocc), 23 fruit (© Brandon Bourdages), 23 leaf (© Radka Palenikova), 24 pine needles (© William Berry), 24 roots (© Maksym Gorpenyuk), 24 trunk (© EastVillage Images), 24 seeds (© Bobkeenan Photography).

Front cover photograph of a tree in fall reproduced with permission of Shutterstock (© sonya etchison). Back cover photograph of a weeping willow tree reproduced with permission of Shutterstock (© Jeff Dalton).

We would like to thank Michael Bright for his invaluable help in the preparation of this book.

Every effort has been made to contact copyright holders of any material reproduced in this book. Any omissions will be rectified in subsequent printings if notice is given to the publisher.

Contents

leaf

bud

Ash

leaf

blossom

Cherry

Dragon's Blood

branch

trunk

6

leaf

bark

Giant Sequoia

Hazel

hazelnut

berry

leaf

Holly

leaf

seed

Horse Chestnut

Monkey Puzzle

branch

leaf

North American Pine

pine needles

Oak

leaf

acorn

14

trunk

fruit

Pear

15

Pussy Willow

leaf

catkin

Silver Birch

trunk

branch

leaf

cone

Spruce

leaf

Seeds

flower

Tulip Tree

catkin

Weeping Willow

Picture Glossary

 **bark** rough, outer covering of a tree

 **berry** small, round fruit with one seed or lots of seeds inside

 **blossom** flowers that appear on a fruit tree before the fruit

 **branch** part of a tree that grows out of the tree's trunk. Branches help a tree spread its leaves out.

 **bud** part of a plant that grows into a new leaf or a flower

 **catkin** small group of flowers on a short stem that grows on some trees

 **cone** hard case that keeps seeds safe. Fir and pine trees have seed cones.

 **flower** part of a plant that makes seeds. The smells flowers make and their colors help attract insects.

 **fruit** fruits hold seeds. Plants make fruit so that animals will eat the fruit and carry the seeds to new places.

 **leaf** part of a plant. Leaves use sunlight to make food for the plant.

23

 **pine needles** long, thin, pointed leaves

 **roots** part of a plant that holds the plant in the ground. Roots bring water to the plant.

 **seeds** plants make seeds. Seeds grow into new plants.

 **trunk** main stem of a tree

Notes for Parents and Teachers

- Go on a nature walk with the children. Help them identify different trees and their parts. Explain that trees are a type of plant. The children can sketch or photograph what they see. Use the pictures to make a class book.
- Collect different leaves and make some bark rubbings. Discuss the different shapes and colors of leaves, and the different bark patterns. Add the pressed leaves and bark rubbings to the class book. Remind children to always check with an adult that leaves are safe to collect, and to always wash their hands after handling leaves.

24